SELECT COMMITTEE TO INVESTIGATE THE
JANUARY 6TH
ATTACK ON THE UNITED STATES CAPITOL

Select Committee to Investigate the
JANUARY 6TH
Attack on the United States Capitol

Fourth Select Committee Hearing
June 21, 2022

COMPLETE TRANSCRIPT

- As Delivered -

Bennie Thompson: "The Select Committee to investigate the January 6th attack on the United States Capitol will be in order. Without objection, the chair is authorized to declare the committee in recess at any point. Pursuant to House Deposition Authority Regulation 10, the chair announces the committee's approval to release the deposition material presented during today's hearing.

"Good afternoon. In our last hearing, we told a story of a scheme driven by Donald Trump to pressure former Vice President Mike Pence to illegally overturn the election results. We showed that when the pressure campaign failed and Mike Pence fulfilled his constitutional obligation, Donald Trump turned a violent mob loose on him. We showed that the mob came within roughly 40 feet of the vice president. Today we'll show that what happened to Mike Pence wasn't an isolated part of Donald Trump's scheme to overturn the election. In fact, pressuring public servants into betraying their oath was a fundamental part of the playbook, and a handful of election officials in several key states stood between Donald Trump and the upending of American democracy.

"As we meet again today, it's important to remember, when we count the votes for president, we count the votes state by state. For the most part, the candidates who win the popular vote in a state wins all the state's Electoral College votes, and whoever wins a majority of the Electoral College votes wins the presidency. So, when Donald Trump tried to overturn the election results, he focused on just a few states. He wanted officials at the local and state level to say the vote was tainted by widespread fraud and throw out the results even though, as we showed last week, there wasn't any voter fraud that could have overturn the election results. And like Mike

Pence, these public servants wouldn't go along with Donald Trump's scheme.

"And when they wouldn't embrace the big lie and substitute the will of the voters with Donald Trump's will to remain in power, Donald Trump worked to ensure they'd face the consequences; threats to people's livelihood and lives, threats of violence that Donald Trump knew about and amplified.

"And in our other hearings, we can't just look backward at what happened in late 2020 and in early 2021 because the danger hadn't gone away. Our democracy endured a mighty test on January 6th and in the days before. We see our institutions held, but what does that really mean? Democratic institutions aren't abstractions or ideas. playbook, and a handful of election officials in several key states stood between Donald Trump and the upending of American democracy.

"As we meet again today, it's important to remember, when we count the votes for president, we count the votes state by state. For the most part, the candidates who win the popular vote in a state wins all the state's Electoral College votes, and whoever wins a majority of the Electoral College votes wins the presidency.

"So, when Donald Trump tried to overturn the election results, he focused on just a few states. He wanted officials at the local and state level to say the vote was tainted by widespread fraud and throw out the results even though, as we showed last week, there wasn't any voter fraud that could have overturn the election results.

"And like Mike Pence, these public servants wouldn't go along with Donald Trump's scheme. And when they wouldn't embrace the big lie and substitute the will of the voters with Donald Trump's will to remain in power, Donald Trump worked to ensure they'd face the consequences; threats to people's livelihood and lives, threats of violence that Donald Trump knew about and amplified. And in our other hearings, we can't just look backward at what happened in late 2020 and in early 2021 because the danger hadn't gone away. Our democracy endured a mighty test on January 6th and in the days before. We see our institutions held, but what does that really mean? Democratic institutions aren't abstractions or ideas. They are local officials who oversee elections, secretaries of state, people in whom we placed our trust that they'll carry out their duties. But what if they don't?

"Two weeks ago, New Mexico held its primary elections. One county commission refused to certify the results, citing vague, unsupported claims dealing with Dominion voting machines. The court stepped in, saying New Mexico law required the commission to certify the results. Two of the three members of the commission finally relented. One still refused, saying his vote 'Isn't based on any evidence. It's not based on any facts. It's only based on my gut feeling and my own intuition, and that's all I need.' By the way, a few months ago this county commissioner was found guilty of illegally entering the Capitol grounds on January 6th. This story reminds us of a few things.

"First, as we've shown in our previous hearings, claims that widespread voter fraud tainted the 2020 presidential election have always been a lie. Donald Trump knew they were a lie and he kept amplifying them anyway. Everything we describe today, the relentless, destructive pressure campaign on state and local officials, was all based on a lie. Donald Trump knew it. He did it anyway. Second, the lie hasn't gone away. It's corrupting our democratic institutions. People who believe that lie are now seeking positions of public trust. And as seen in New Mexico, their oath to be — to the people they serve will take a back seat to their commitment to the big lie. If that happens, who will make sure our institutions don't break under the pressure? We won't have close calls. We'll have a catastrophe.

"My distinguished colleague from California, Mr. Schiff, will present much of the Select Committee's findings on this matter. First, I'm pleased to recognize our vice chair, Ms. Cheney, of Wyoming for any opening statement she'd care to offer."

Liz Cheney: "Thank you very much, Mr. Chairman. Today we will begin examining President Trump's effort to overturn the election by exerting pressure on state officials and state legislatures. Donald Trump had a direct and personal role in this effort, as did Rudy Giuliani, as did John Eastman. In other words, the same people who were attempting to pressure Vice President Mike Pence to reject electoral votes illegally were also simultaneously working to reverse the outcome of the 2020 election at the state level. Each of these efforts to overturn the election is independently serious. Each deserves attention, both by Congress and by our Department of Justice. But as a federal court has already indicated, these efforts were also part of a broader plan, and all of this was done in preparation for January 6th. I would note two points for particular focus today.

"First, today you will hear about calls made by President Trump to officials of Georgia and other states. As you listen to these tapes, keep in mind what Donald Trump already knew at the time he was making those calls. He had been told over and over again that his stolen election allegations were nonsense. For example, this is what former Attorney General Bill Barr said to President Trump about allegations in Georgia."

> **[multimedia]**
> **William Barr: "We took a look — a hard look at this ourselves. And based on our review of it, including the interviews of the key**

witnesses, the Fulton County allegations were — had no merit. They're — the — the ballots under the table were legitimate ball — ballots. They weren't in a suitcase. They had been pre-opened for eventually feeding into the machinc, all the stuff about the water leak and that there was some subterfuge involved. We felt there was some confusion, but — but there was no evidence of a subterfuge to create an opportunity to feed things into the count. And so, we didn't see any evidence of — of fraud in the — in the Fulton County episode."

Liz Cheney: "And Acting Deputy Attorney General Richard Donoghue told Donald Trump this."

[multimedia]
Richard Donoghue: "And I said something to the effect of, sir, we've done dozens of investigations, hundreds of interviews. The major allegations are not supported by the evidence developed."

Liz Cheney: "Mr. Trump was told by his own advisers that he had no basis for his stolen election claims, yet he continued to pressure state officials to change the election results. Second, you will hear about a number of threats and efforts to pressure state officials to reverse the election outcome. One of our witnesses today, Gabriel Sterling, explicitly warned President Trump about potential violence on December 1st, 2020, more than a month before January 6th. You will see excerpts from that video repeatedly today."

[multimedia]
Gabriel Sterling: "It has all gone to bar. All of it. Joe diGenova [ph] today askcd for Chrls Krebs, a patriot who ran CISA, to be shot. A 20 something tech in Gwinnett County today

has death threats and a noose put out saying he should be hung for treason because he was transferring a report on batches from an EMS to a county computer, so he could read it. It has to stop. Mr. President, you have not condemned these actions or this language. Senators, you have not condemned this language or these actions. This has to stop. We need you to step up. And if you're gonna take a position of leadership, show some. My boss, Secretary Raffensperger, his address is out there. They have people doing caravans in front of their house. They've had people come on to their property. It has to stop. This is elections. This is the backbone of democracy. And all of you who have not said a damn word are complicit in this."

Liz Cheney: "The point is this, Donald Trump did not care about the threats of violence. He did not condemn them. He made no effort to stop them. He went forward with his fake allegations anyway. One more point, I would urge all of those watching today to focus on the evidence the committee will present. Don't be distracted by politics. This is serious. We cannot let America become a nation of conspiracy theories and thug violence. Finally, I want to thank our witnesses today for all of your service to our country. Today, all of America will hear about the selfless actions of these men and women who acted honorably to uphold the law, protect our freedom, and preserve our Constitution. Today, Mr. Chairman, we will all see an example of what truly makes America great. Thank you. Mr. Chairman, I yield back."

Bennie Thompson: "Without objection, the Chair recognizes the gentleman from California, Mr. Schiff, for an opening statement."

Adam Schiff: "Thank you, Mr. Chairman and Madam Vice Chair. On November 3rd, 2020, Donald Trump ran for eelection to the office of the presidency and he lost. His opponent, Joe Biden, finished ahead in the key battleground states of Arizona, Michigan, Wisconsin, Pennsylvania, Georgia, and elsewhere. Nevertheless, and for the first time in history, the losing Presidential candidate fought to hold on to power. As we have seen in previous hearings, he did so through a variety of means. On Election Day, he sought to stop the counting of the vote knowing that the millions of absentee ballots elections officials would be counting on Election Day and thereafter would run strongly against him and deliver a victory to Joe Biden.

"Next, and when he could not stop the counting, he tried to stop state legislatures and governors from certifying the results of the election. He went to court and filed dozens of frivolous lawsuits making unsubstantiated claims of fraud. When that too failed, he mounted a pressure campaign directed at individual state legislators to try to get them to go back into session and either declare him the winner, decertify Joe Biden as the winner, or send two slates of electors to Congress, one for Biden and one for him and pressure Vice President Pence to choose him as the winner. But the state legislatures wouldn't go along with this scheme and neither would the Vice President.

"None of the legislatures agreed to go back in the special session and declare him the winner. No legitimate state authority in the states Donald Trump lost would agree to appoint fake Trump electors and send them to Congress. But this didn't stop the Trump campaign either. They assembled groups of individuals in key battleground states and got them to call themselves electors, created phony certificates associated with these fake electors, and then transmitted these certificates to Washington and to the Congress to be counted during the joint session of Congress on January 6th. None of this worked, but according to federal District Judge David Carter, former President Trump and others likely violated multiple federal laws by engaging in this scheme, including conspiracy to defraud the United States.

"You will hear evidence of the former President and his top adviser's direct involvement in key elements of this plot, or what Judge Carter called a coup, in search of a legal theory. Or as the judge explained, 'President Trump's pressure campaign to stop the electoral count did not end with Vice President Pence. It targeted every tier of federal and state elected officials. Convincing state legislatures', he said, 'to certify competing electors was essential to stop the count and ensure President Trump's reelection.'

"As we have seen in our prior hearings. Running through this scheme was a big lie that the election was plagued with massive fraud and somehow stolen. You'll remember what President — the President's own attorney general, Bill Barr said, he told the President about these claims of massive fraud affecting the outcome of the election."

> [multimedia]
> **William Barr: "And I told him that the stuff that his people were shoveling out to the public or bull — was bullshit. I mean that the claims of fraud were bullshit."**

Adam Schiff: "The President's lie was and is a dangerous cancer on the body politic. If you can convince Americans that they cannot trust their own elections, that any time they lose it is somehow illegitimate, then what is left but violence to determine who should govern. This brings us to the focus of today's hearing. When state elections officials refused to stop the count, Donald Trump and his campaign tried to put pressure on them. When state executive officials refused to certify him the winner of states he lost, he applied more pressure. When state legislators refused to go back into session and appoint

Trump electors, he amped up the pressure yet again. Anyone who got in the way of Donald Trump's continued hold on power after he lost the election was the subject of a dangerous and escalating campaign of pressure.

This pressure campaign brought angry phone calls and texts, armed protests, intimidation, and all too often threats of violence and death. State legislators were singled out. So too were statewide elections officials. Even local elections workers diligently doing their jobs were accused of being criminals and had their lives turned upside down. As we will show, the President's supporters heard the former President's claims of fraud and the false allegations he made against state and local officials as a call to action."

[multimedia]

Unknown: "Stop the steal. Stop the steal. Stop the steal. [inaudible] You're a threat to democracy. [inaudible] You're a threat to free and honest election. We love America. We love our rights and our freedom. [inaudible] You are a tyrant, you are a felon and you must turn yourself into authorities immediately. [inaudible]"

Jocelyn Benson: "And then about 45 minutes later, we started to hear the noises outside my home. And that's why my stomach sank. And I thought, it's me. And there — and then it's just we don't know what's gonna — the uncertainty of that was what was the fear. Are they coming with guns? Are they going to attack my House? I'm in here with my kid. You know, I'm trying to put him to bed. And so it was — yeah, that was the scariest moment just not knowing what was going to happen."

Adam Schiff: "This pressure campaign against state and local officials spanned numerous contested states as you will see in this video produced by the Select Committee."

[multimedia]

Josh Roselman: "My name is Josh Roselman. I'm an investigative counsel for the House Select Committee to investigate the January 6th attack on the United States Capitol. Beginning in late November 2020, the President and his lawyers started appearing before state legislators urging them to give their electoral votes to Trump even though he lost the popular vote."

Rudy Giuliani: "I represent President Trump along with Jenna Ellis. And this is our fourth or fifth hearing."

Donald Trump: "This election has to be turned around because we won Pennsylvania by a lot and we won all of these swing states by a lot."

Josh Roselman: "This was a strategy with both practical and legal elements. The Select Committee has obtained an email from just two days after the election in which a Trump campaign lawyer named Cleta Mitchell asked another Trump lawyer, John Eastman, to write a memo justifying the idea."

Unknown: "When do you remember this coming up as an option in the post-election period for the first time?"

Cleta Mitchell: "Right after the election. It might have been before the election."

Josh Roselman: "Eastman prepared a memo attempting to justify this strategy, which was circulated to the Trump White House, Rudy Giuliani's legal team, and state legislators around the country. And he appeared before the Georgia state legislature to advocate for it publicly."

John Eastman: "She could also do what the Florida legislature was prepared to do, which is to adopt a slate of electors yourselves. And when you add in the mix of the significant statistical anomalies in sworn [affidavits] and video evidence of outright election fraud, I don't think it's just your authority to do that. But quite frankly, I think you have a duty to do that, to protect the integrity of — of the election here in Georgia."

Josh Roselman: "But Republican officials in several states released public statements recognizing that President Trump's proposal was unlawful. For instance, Georgia Governor Brian Kemp called the proposal unconstitutional. While Arizona House Speaker Rusty Bowers wrote that the idea would undermine the rule of law. The pressure campaign to get state legislators to go along with the scheme intensified when President Trump invited delegations from Michigan and Pennsylvania to the White House."

Unknown: "Either you or Speaker Chatfield, did you make the point to the President that you were not going to do anything that violated Michigan law?"

Mike Shirkey: "I believe we did. Whether or not was those exact words or not, we're   I think the words that I would have more likely used is we are going to follow the law."

Josh Roselman: "Nevertheless, the pressure continued. The next day President Trump tweeted quote, 'Hopefully the courts and or legislatures will have the courage to do what has to be done to maintain the integrity of our elections and the United States of America itself. The world is watching.' He posted multiple messages on Facebook, listing the contact information for state officials and urging his supporters to contact them to quote, 'Demand a vote on decertification.' In one of those posts, President Trump disclosed Mike Shirkey's personal phone number to his millions of followers."

Mike Shirkey: "All I remember is receiving over just shy of 4,000 text messages over a short period of time calling to take action. It was a loud noise, loud consistent cadence of, you know, we hear that — that the Trump folks are calling and asking for changes in the electors and you guys can do this. Well, you know they were — they were believing things that were untrue."

Josh Roselman: "These efforts also involved targeted outreach to state legislators."

Angela McCallum: "Hi, Representative. My name is Angela McCallum. I'm calling from Trump campaign headquarters in Washington DC. You do have the power to reclaim your authority and send a — a slate of electors that will support President Trump and Vice President Pence."

Josh Roselman: "From President Trump's lawyers and from Trump himself."

Donald Trump: "And I've become friendly with legislators that I didn't know four weeks ago."

Josh Roselman: "Another legislator, Pennsylvania House Speaker Bryan Cutler, received daily voicemails from Trump's lawyers in the last week of November."

Rudy Giuliani : "Mr. Speaker, this is Rudy Giuliani and Jenna Ellis. We're calling you together because we'd like to discuss obviously the election."

Jenna Ellis: "Hello, Mr. Speaker. This is Jenna Ellis and I'm here with Mayor Giuliani."

Rudy Giuliani: "Hey, Bryan. It's Rudy. I really have something important to call to your attention that I think really changes things."

Josh Roselman: "Cutler felt that the outreach was inappropriate and asked his lawyers to tell Rudy Giuliani to stop calling. But Giuliani continued to reach out."

Rudy Giuliani: "I understand that you don't want to talk to me now. I just want to bring some facts to your attention and talk to you as a fellow Republican."

Josh Roselman: "On December 30th Trump ally Steve Bannon announced a protest at Cutler's home."

Steve Bannon: "We're getting on the road and we're going down to Cutler. We're going to start going to offices. And if we have to we're going to go to homes and we're going to let them know what we think about them."

Bryan Cutler: "There were multiple protests. I actually don't remember the exact number. There was at least three, I think, outside of either my district office or my home. And you're correct, my son — my then 15 year old son was home by himself for the first one. All of my personal information was doxxed online. It was my personal email, my personal cell phone, my home phone number. In fact, we had to disconnect our home phone for about three days because it would ring all hours of the night and would fill up with messages."

Unknown: "Bryan Cutler, we are outside. Clerks facing felony charges in Michigan. Poll watchers denied access in Pennsylvania –"

Josh Roselman: "— These ads were another element in the effort. The Trump campaign spent millions of dollars running ads online and on television."

Unknown: "The evidence is overwhelming. Call your governor and legislators. Demand they inspect the machines and hear the evidence."

Josh Roselman: "Public pressure on state officials often grew dangerous in the lead up to January 6th."

Unknown: "Let us in. Let us in. Let us in. Special session. Special session. Special session. We'll light the whole shit on fire."

Nick Fuentes: "What are we going to do? What can you and I do to a state legislator besides kill him? Although, we should not do that. I'm not advising that, but I mean what else can you do? Right?"

Unknown: "The punishment for treason is death."

Adam Schiff: "The state pressure campaign and the danger it posed to state officials and to State Capitols around the nation was a dangerous precursor to the violence we saw on January 6th at the US Capitol. Today you will hear from Rusty Bowers, the Republican Speaker of the Arizona House of Representatives. He will tell us about his conversations with the President, with Rudy Giuliani, and John Eastman, and what the President's team asked of him and how his oath of office would not permit it. You will then hear from Brad Raffensperger, the Republican Secretary of state of Georgia who Trump directed to quote, 'Find 11,780 votes' that did not exist, but just the exact number of votes needed to overtake Joe Biden.

"You will also hear from Gabriel Sterling, the Chief Operating Officer — his Chief Operating Officer, about the spurious claims of fraud in the elections in Georgia and who, responding to a cascading set of threats to his elections team, warned the President to stop, that someone was going to get killed. And you will hear from Wandrea — Wandrea 'Shaye' Moss, a former local elections worker in Fulton County, Georgia, about how all of the lies about the election impacted the lives of real people who administer our elections and still do. You will hear what they experienced when the most powerful man in the world, the President of the United States, sought to cling to power after being voted out of office by the American people. The system held, but barely. And the system held because people of courage, Republicans and Democrats, like the witnesses you will hear today put their oath to the country and constitution above any other consideration. They did their jobs as we must do ours. Thank you, Mr. Chairman. And I yield back."

Bennie Thompson: "I now welcome our first panel of witnesses. We're joined today by a distinguished legislator from Arizona, Rusty Bowers, who's a Republican Speaker of the Arizona House of Representatives. Mr. Bower was first elected to the state legislature in 1993 and has served as Speaker since 2019. Welcome, Speaker Bowers. Brad Raffensperger is the 29th Secretary of State of Georgia, serving in this role since 2019. As an elected official and a Republican, Secretary Raffensperger is responsible for supervising elections in Georgia and maintaining the state's public records. Welcome, Mr. Secretary. Gabriel Sterling is the Chief Operating Officer in the Georgia Secretary of State's office.

"Mr. Sterling was the statewide voting systems implementation manager for the 2020 election in Georgia, responsible for leading the Secretary of State's response to the COVID pandemic and rolling out modernized voting equipment. I will swear in our witnesses. The witnesses will please stand and raise their right hand. Do you swear or inform — form under the penalty of perjury that the testimony you're about to give is the truth, the whole truth, and nothing but the truth so help you God? Thank you. Please be seated.

"Let the record reflect that the witnesses answered in the affirmative. Speaker Bowers, thank you for being with us today. You're the Speaker of the Arizona House and a self-described conservative Republican. You campaigned for President Trump and with him during the 2020 election. Is it fair to say that you wanted Donald Trump to win a second term in office? Please."

Rusty Bowers: "Yes, Sir. Thank you."

Bennie Thompson: "And is it your understanding that President Biden was the winner of the popular vote in Arizona in 2020?"

Rusty Bowers: "Yes, sir."

Bennie Thompson: "Thank you. Pursuant to Section five C8 of House Resolution 503, the Chair recognizes the gentleman from California, Mr. Schiff for questions."

Adam Schiff: "Speaker Bowers, thank you for being with us today. Before we begin with the questions that I have prepared for you, I wanted to ask you about a statement that former President Trump issued which I received just prior to the hearing. Have you had a chance to review that statement?"

Rusty Bowers: "I — my counsel called from Arizona and read it to me. Yes, Sir."

Adam Schiff: "In that statement — I won't read it in its entirety — former President Trump begins by calling you a RINO, Republican in name only. He then references a conversation in November 2020 in which he claims that you told him that the election was rigged and that he had won Arizona. To quote the former President, 'During the conversation he told me the election was rigged and that I won Arizona unquote.' Did you have such a conversation with the President?"

Rusty Bowers: "I did have a conversation with the President. That's certainly isn't it. But there are parts of it that are true, but there are parts that are not, Sir."

Adam Schiff: "And the part that I read to you, is that false?"

Rusty Bowers: "Anywhere, anyone, any time has said that I said the election was rigged, that would not be true."

Adam Schiff: "And when the Pre — the former President in his statement today claimed that you told him that he won Arizona, is that also false?"

Rusty Bowers: "That is also false."

Adam Schiff: "Mr. Bowers, I understand that after the election — and I don't know whether this is the conversation the former President is referring to — but after the election you received a phone call from President Trump and Rudy Giuliani in which they discussed the result of the Presidential election in Arizona. If you would, tell us about that call and whether the former President or Mr. Giuliani raised allegations of election fraud."

Rusty Bowers: "Thank you. I — my wife and I had returned from attending our church meetings. It was on a Sunday. And we were still in the driveway. And I had received a call from a colleague telling me that the White House was trying to get in touch with her and I. And that she said please if you get a call, let's try to take this together.

"Immediately I saw that the White House on my Bluetooth was calling and I took the call and was asked by the — I would presume the operator at the White House if I would hold for the President, which I did. And he — Mr. Giuliani came on first, and niceties. Then Mr. Trump — President Trump – then President Trump came on and we initiated a conversation."

Adam Schiff: "And during that conversation did you ask Mr. Giu — Giuliani for proof of these allegations of fraud that he was making?"

Rusty Bowers: "On multiple occasions, yes."

Adam Schiff: "And when you asked him for evidence of this fraud what did he say?"

Rusty Bowers: "He said that they did have proof. And I asked him, do you have names? For example, we have 200,000 illegal immigrants, some large number. Five or 6,000 dead people, et cetera. And I said, do you have their names? Yes? Will you give them to me? Yes. The President interrupted and said give the man what he needs, Rudy. And he said I — I will. And that happened on at least two occasions, that interchange in the conversation."

Adam Schiff: "So Mr. Giuliani was claiming in the call that there were hundreds of thousands of undocumented people and thousands of dead people who had purportedly voted in the election?"

Rusty Bowers: "Yes."

Adam Schiff: "And you asked him for evidence of that."

Rusty Bowers: "I did."

Adam Schiff: "And did he ever receive — did you ever receive from him that evidence either during the call after the call or to this day?"

Rusty Bowers: "Never."

Adam Schiff: "What was the ask during this call? He was making these allegations of fraud, but he had something or a couple of things that they wanted you to do. What were those?"

Rusty Bowers: "The ones I remember were first the — that we would hold — that I would allow an official committee at — at the Capitol so that they could hear this evidence and that we could take action thereafter. And I refused. I said up to that time the — the circus — I called it a circus — had been brewing with lots of demonstrations both at the counting center, at the Capitol, and other places.

"And I didn't want to have that in the House. I — I did not feel that the evidence granted in its absence merited a hearing. And I didn't want to be used as a pawn. If there was some other need that the – that the committee hearing would fulfill. So, that was the first ask, that we hold an official committee hearing."

Adam Schiff: "And what was his second ask?"

Rusty Bowers: "I — I said to what end? To what end the hearing? He said, well, we have heard by an official high up in the Republican legislature that there is a legal theory or a legal ability in Arizona that you can remove the — the electors of President Biden and replace them. And we would — we would like to have the legitimate opportunity through the committee to come to that end and — and remove that. And I said that's — that's something I've — that's totally new to me. I've never heard of any such thing. And he pressed that point. And I said, look, you are asking me to do something that is counter to my oath when I swore to the Constitution to uphold it, and I also swore to the Constitution and the laws of the state of Arizona.

"And this is totally foreign as a — an idea or a theory to me, and I would never do anything of such magnitude without deep consultation with qualified attorneys. And I said I've got some good attorneys and I'm going to give you their names, but you are asking me to do something against my oath, and I will not break my oath. And I think that was up to that point."

Adam Schiff: "During the conversation — and you heard, I think, when we played a snippet of Mr. Giuliani calling other state legislators and saying that he was calling as essentially a fellow Republican. Did he make a similar appeal to you, or bring up the fact that you shared a — a similar party?"

Rusty Bowers: "Whether it was in that call or in a later meeting, he did bring that up more than once."

Adam Schiff: "And how — how would he bring that up?"

Rusty Bowers: "He would say, aren't we all Republicans here? I — I would think we would get a better reception. I mean, I would think you would listen a little more open to my suggestions, that we're all Republicans."

Adam Schiff: "And this — this evidence that you asked him for that would justify this extraordinary step I think you said they never produced. Why did you feel, either in the absence of that evidence or with it, what they were asking you to do would violate your oath to the Constitution?"

Rusty Bowers: "First of all, when the people — and in Arizona, I believe it — some 40-plus years earlier the legislature had established the manner of electing our officials or the electors for the presidential race. Once it was given to the people as in Bush v Gore, illustrated by the Supreme Court, it becomes a fundamental right of the people. So, as far as I was concerned, for someone to ask me in the — I would call it a paucity. There was no – no evidence being presented of any strength.

"Evidence can be hearsay evidence. It's still evidence, but it's still hearsay. But strong judicial quality evidence, anything that would say to me you have a doubt, deny your oath, I will not do that. And on more than — on more than one occasion throughout all this, that has been brought up. And it is a tenet of my faith that the Constitution is divinely inspired, of my most basic foundational beliefs. And so, for me to do that because somebody just asked me to is foreign to my very being. I — I will not do it."

Adam Schiff: "During that conversation, Speaker Bowers, did you ask him if what he was proposing had ever been done before?"

Rusty Bowers: "I did."

Adam Schiff: "And what did he say?"

Rusty Bowers: "He said, well, I'm not familiar with Arizona law or any other laws, but I — I don't — I don't think so.

"And that also was brought up in other conversations, both with him and with John Eastman and others."

Adam Schiff: "Speaker Bowers, I understand that a week after that call, Mr. Giuliani appeared with others associated with President Trump's effort to overturn the result of the election at a purported legislative hearing in a hotel ballroom in Phoenix. Was this an official hearing of the state legislature?"

Rusty Bowers: "It was not."

Adam Schiff: "And — and why was it not a real or official hearing of the legislature?"

Rusty Bowers: "A legislator can hold a group meeting. You can call it a hearing. But when they asked me to have an official hearing, we establish it by protocols, public notice, etc. It's typically held at the Capitol, but doesn't need to be. We can authorize a hearing off campus. And in this case, I had been asked on several occasions to allow a hearing. I had denied it, but said you're free to hold a meeting, any meeting you want, to the person who asked, and which he ultimately did. I think he was a little frustrated, but he ultimately did."

Adam Schiff: "Now, this — this meeting was the same day, I believe, that the governor of Arizona, Doug Ducey, certified Biden as the winner of the presidential election in Arizona. Did you meet with Mr. Giuliani and his associates while they were in Phoenix sometime after that purported legislative hearing at the hotel?"

Rusty Bowers: "Yes, I did, sir."

Adam Schiff: "And at that meeting, did Mr. Giuliani raise any specific allegations of election fraud again?"

Rusty Bowers: "His initial comments were, again, the litany of groups of illegal individuals or people deceased, etc. And he had brought that up, and I wasn't alone in that meeting. There were others, and other members of the Senate aggressively questioned him, and then I proceeded to question him on the proof that he was going to bring me, etc. But he did bring those up, yes."

Adam Schiff: "And these other legislatures — legislators were also Republican members of the Senate?"

Rusty Bowers: "They were, yes, sir."

Adam Schiff: "And did they also press him for proof of these allegations?"

Rusty Bowers: "And they pressed him very strongly, two of them especially, very strongly."

Adam Schiff: "And at some point, did Mr. Giuliani ask one of the other attorneys on his team to help him out with the evidence?"

Rusty Bowers: "He did. He asked Jenna Ellis, who was sitting to his right. One thing was that it was more to the point of was there sufficient evidence or action that we could justify the recalling of the electors. But at that part of the conversation, I know he — he referred to someone else. But he did ask, do we have the proof to Jenna, Ms. Ellis, and she said yes.

"And I said I want the names. Do you have the names? Yes. Do you have how they voted? We have all the information. I said, can you get to me that information? Did you bring it with you? Just — she said no. Both Mr. Giuliani asked her and I asked generally if they had brought it with them. She said no, it's not with me, but we can get it to you. And I said then you didn't bring me the evidence, which was repeated in different iterations for some period of time."

Adam Schiff: "At some point, did one of them make a comment that they didn't have evidence, but they had a lot of theories?"

Rusty Bowers: "That was Mr. Giuliani. And what exactly did he say and how'd that come up? My recollection, he said we've got lots of theories. We just don't have the evidence. And I don't know if that was a gaffe or maybe he — he didn't think through what he said. But both myself and others in my group, the three in my group and my — my counsel, both remembered that specifically, and afterwards we kind of laughed about it."

Adam Schiff: "And, you know, getting back to the ask in that phone call that preceded this meeting, he wanted you to have the legislature dismiss the Biden electors and replace them with Trump electors on the basis of these theories of fraud."

Rusty Bowers: "I — he did not say in those exact words, but he did say that he — that Arizona law, according to what he understood, that that would be allowed and that we needed to come into session to take care of that, which initiated a discussion about, again, what I can legally and not legally do. And I can't go into session in Arizona unilaterally or on my sole prerogative."

Adam Schiff: "In this meeting or at any other later time, did anyone provide you with evidence of election fraud sufficient to affect the outcome of the presidential election in Arizona?"

Rusty Bowers: "No one provided me, ever, such evidence."

Adam Schiff: "The Select Committee has uncovered evidence in the course of our investigation that at stop the steal protests at state capitols across the country, there were individuals with ties to the groups or parties involved in the January 6th attack on the US Capitol. One of those incursions took place in the Arizona House of Representatives building, as you can see in this footage.

"This is previously undisclosed video of protesters illegally entering and refusing to leave the building. One of the individuals prominently shown in this video is Jacob Chansley, perhaps better known as the QAnon Shaman. This rioter entered the Capitol on January 6th, was photographed leaving a threatening note on the dais in the US Senate chamber, and was ultimately sentenced to 41 months in prison after pleading guilty to obstruction of an official proceeding. Other protesters who occupied the Arizona House of Representatives building included — included Proud Boys, while men armed with rifles stood just outside the entrance. I understand these protesters were calling for you by name, Speaker Bowers. Is that correct?"

Rusty Bowers: "That is correct."

Adam Schiff: "Speaker Bowers, did the president call you again in late — later in December?"

Rusty Bowers: "He did, sir."

Adam Schiff: "And did you tell the president in that second call that you supported him, that you voted for him, but that you were not going to do anything illegal for him?"

Rusty Bowers: "I did, sir."

Adam Schiff: "Nevertheless, his lawyer, John Eastman, called you some days later on June 4th, 2000 — 2021. And he did have a very specific ask that would have required you to do just what you had already told the president, you wouldn't do, something that would violate your oath. Is that correct?"

Rusty Bowers: "That's correct. It wasn't just me. I had my counsel and others on the — on the — on the call."

Adam Schiff: "And what did Dr. Eastman want you to do?"

Rusty Bowers: "That we would in fact vote — to take a vote to overthrow or — I shouldn't say overthrow, that we would decertify the electors, and that that — because we had plenary authority to do so. And you cited Article Two, Section One, I think it's Clause Two, and said that in his opinion that gave us the authority if there was — I don't recall him saying sufficient evidence, but there was some call or some strong reason to do so, that we — or justification to do so, that we could do that.

"And that he was asking that we — he's — his suggestion was that we would do it. And I said, again, I took an oath. For me to take that, to do what you do, would — would be counter to my oath. I don't recall if it was in that conversation clearly that we talked more about the oath. But I said, what would you have me do? And he said just do it and let the court sort it out. And I said you're asking me to do something that's never been done in history, the history of the United States. And I'm going to put my state through that without sufficient proof, and that's going to be good enough with me? That I would — I would put us through that, my state, that I swore to uphold both in Constitution and in law?

"No, sir. He said, well, that's — my suggestion would be just — just do it and let the courts figure it all out. And I — he didn't use that exact phrase, but that was what he — his meaning was. And I said — I declined, and I believe that was close to the end of our phone call."

Adam Schiff: "And again, this took place after you had recently spoken with President Trump and told him that you wouldn't do anything illegal for him. Is that right?"

Rusty Bowers: "It wasn't days after. Obviously, it was days after, but a few days had gone by."

Adam Schiff: "But you had told President Trump you would not do anything illegal for him?"

Rusty Bowers: "I did both times."

Adam Schiff: "And you told Dr. Eastman that you did not believe there was legal support to justify what he was asking, but he still wanted you to do it and effectively let the courts work it out."

Rusty Bowers: "I've been warned don't say things you think maybe he said. But I do remember him saying that the authority of the legislature was plenary, and that you can do it. I said then you should know that I can't even call the legislature into session without a two-thirds majority vote. We're only 30 plus one. I --there's no way that could happen."

Adam Schiff: "But in your view, what he was asking you to do would have violated your oath to the Constitution, both the United States Constitution and the Constitution of the state of Arizona?"

Rusty Bowers: "Yes, sir."

Adam Schiff: "Did you also receive a call from US Representative Andy Biggs of Arizona on the morning of January 6th?"

Rusty Bowers: "I did."

Adam Schiff: "And what did Mr. Biggs ask you to do?"

Rusty Bowers: "I believe that was the day that the vote was occurring to each state certification or to declare that the certification of the electors. And he asked if I would sign on both to a letter that had been sent from my state and/or that I would support the decertification of the electors. And I said I would not."

Adam Schiff: "Mr. Speaker, on December 4th, 2020, shortly after your meeting with Rudy Giuliani and other allies of President Trump, you released a statement publicly addressing quote, 'calls for the legislature to overturn the 2020 certified election results'. The statement is very straightforward in explaining the quote, 'breathtaking request', unquote made by representatives of President Trump quote, 'that the Arizona legislature overturn the certified results of last month's election and deliver the state's Electoral College votes to President Trump', unquote. Why did you believe as you wrote in this statement that the rule of law forbid you from doing what President Trump and his allies wanted you to do?"

Rusty Bowers: "Representative — I'm sorry, I should be saying Mr. Chairman — Representative Schiff. The — there's two sides to the answer. One is, what am I allowed to do? And, what am I forbidden to do? We have no legal pathway, both in state law nor to my knowledge in federal law, for us to execute such a request. And I am not allowed to walk or act beyond my authority if I'm not specifically authorized as a legislator — as a legislature, then I cannot act to the point of calling us into session. Some say that just a few legislators have plenary author — authority and that is come — is part of all of this discussion, I'll call it. But — so to — to not have authority and be forbidden to act beyond my authority, on both counts, I'm not authorized to take such action, and that would deny my oath."

Adam Schiff: "In your statement, you included excerpts from President Ronald Reagan's inaugural address in 1981. The newly inaugurated President told the country quote, 'the orderly transfer of authority is called for in the Constitution routinely takes place as is — as it has for almost two centuries. And few of us stop to think how unique we really are. In the eyes of many in the world, this every four year ceremony we accept as normal is nothing less than a miracle.' Tell us, if you would, Mr. Speaker, why did you include President Reagan's words in your public statement?"

Rusty Bowers: "Mr. Chairman, Representative Schiff, because I have a lot of admiration for Ronald Reagan. I had the opportunity of going to his home with one other person and walking through. And I have a lot of admiration for him. When he pointed out, which is I — I have lived in other country for a period of time and have visited a few countries and during election times. The fact that we allow an election, support an election, and stand behind the election, even in the past when there have been serious questions about the election and then move on without disturbance and with acceptance that we choose — we choose to follow the outcome of the will of the people. That will, it means a lot to me and I know it meant a lot to him, and so I — we included that."

Adam Schiff: "Thank you, Speaker Bowers. And I want to look even more deeply at the fake elector scheme. Every four years, citizens from all over the United States go to the polls to elect their President. Under our Constitution, when we cast our votes for President, we are actually voting to send electors pledged to our preferred candidate to the Electoral College. In December, the electors in each state meet, cast their votes, and send those votes to Washington. There is only one legitimate slate of electors from each state. On the sixth day of January, Congress meets in a joint session to count those votes and the winner of the Electoral College vote becomes the President.

"In this next segment, you'll hear how President Trump and his campaign were directly involved in advancing and coordinating the plot to replace legitimate Biden electors with fake electors not chosen by the voters. You'll hear how this campaign convinced these fake electors to cast and submit their votes through fake certificates telling them that their votes would only be used in the event that President Trump won his legal challenges.

"Yet, when the President lost those legal challenges, when courts rejected them as frivolous and without merit, the fake elector scheme continued. At this point, President Trump's own lawyers, so- called team normal, walked away rather than participate in the plan. And his own White House counsel's office said that the plan was not legally sound. Let's play the following video produced by the Select Committee."

[multimedia]

<u>Casey Lucier</u>: "My name is Casey Lucier. I'm an investigative counsel for the House Select Committee to investigate the January 6th attack on the United States Capitol. On November 18th, a lawyer working with the Trump campaign, named Kenneth Chesebro, wrote a memo arguing that the Trump campaign should organize its own electors in the swing states that President Trump had lost. The Select Committee received testimony that those close to President Trump began planning to organize fake electors for Trump in states that Biden won in the weeks after the election."

<u>Unknown</u>: "Who do you remember being involved in those early discussions around the Thanksgiving time regarding having alternate electors meet?"

<u>Cassidy Hutchinson</u>: "Mr. Giuliani, several of Mr. Giuliani's associates, Mr. Meadows, Members of Congress. Although it's difficult to distinguish if the members I'm thinking of were involved during Thanksgiving or if they're involved as we progressed through December."

<u>Casey Lucier</u>: "At the President's direct request, the RNC assisted the campaign in coordinating this effort."

<u>Unknown</u>: "What did the President say when he called you?"

<u>Ronna Romney McDaniel</u>: "Essentially, he turned the call over to Mr. Eastman who then proceeded to talk about the importance of the

RNC helping the campaign gather these contingent electors in case any of the legal challenges that were ongoing changed the result of any of states [ph]. I think more just helping them reach out and assemble them. But that — my understanding is the campaign did take the lead and we just were helping them in that - - in that role."

Casey Lucier: "As President Trump and his supporters continued to lose lawsuits, some campaign lawyers became convinced that convening electors in states that Trump lost was no longer appropriate."

Justin Clark: "I just remember I either replied or called somebody saying, unless we have litigation pending this, like, in these states, like, I don't think this is appropriate or, you know, this isn't the right thing to do. I don't remember how I phrased it, but I got into a little bit of a back and forth and I think it was with Ken Chesebro, where I said, Alright, you know, you just get after it, like, I'm out."

Matt Morgan: "At that point, I had Josh Finley email Mr. Chesebro politely to say this is your task. You are responsible for the Electoral College issues moving forward. And this was my way of taking that responsibility to zero."

Casey Lucier: "The committee learned the White House counsel's office also felt the plan was potentially illegal."

Unknown: "And so to be clear, did you hear the White House counsel's office say that this plan to have alternate electors meet and cast votes for Donald Trump in states that he had lost was not legally sound?"

Cassidy Hutchinson: "Yes, sir."

Unknown: "And who was present for that meeting that you remember?"

Cassidy Hutchinson: "It was in our offices. Mr. Meadows, Mr. Giuliani, and a few of Mr. Giuliani's associates."

Casey Lucier: "The Select Committee interviewed several of the individual fake electors as well as Trump campaign staff who helped organize the effort."

Robert Sinners: "We were just, you know, kind of — kind of useful idiots or rubes at that point. You know, a strong part of me really feels that it's just kind of as the road continued and as that was failure, failure, failure that that got formulated as what we have on the table. Let's just do it."

Unknown: "And now after what we've told you today about the committee's investigation, about the conclusion of the professional lawyers on the campaign staff, Justin Clark, Matt Morgan, and Josh Finley, about their unwillingness to participate in the convening of these electors, how does that contribute to your understanding of these issues?"

Robert Sinners: "I'm angry. I'm angry because I think — I think in a sense, you know, no one really cared if — if people were potentially putting themselves in jeopardy."

Unknown: "Would you have not wanted to participate in this any further as well?"

Robert Sinners: "I absolutely would not have had I known that the three main lawyers for the campaign that I'd spoken to in the past and were leading up were not on board. Yeah."

Andrew Hitt: "I was told that these would only count if a court ruled in our favor. So that would have been using our electors — well, it would have been using our electors in ways that we weren't told about and we wouldn't have supported."

Casey Lucier: "Documents obtained by the Select Committee indicate that instructions were given to the electors in several states that they needed to cast their ballots in complete secrecy. Because this scheme involved fake electors, those participating in certain states had no way to comply with state election laws like where the electors were supposed to meet. One group of fake electors even considered hiding overnight to ensure that they could access the state capital as required in Michigan."

Unknown: "Did Mr. Norton say who he was working with at all on this effort to have electors meet?"

Laura Cox: "He said he was working with the President's campaign. He told me that the Michigan Republican electors were planning to meet in the Capitol and hide overnight so that they could fulfill the role of casting their vote in — per law in the Michigan chambers. And I told him in no uncertain terms that that was insane and inappropriate."

Casey Lucier: "In one state, the fake electors even asked for a promise that the campaign would pay their legal fees if they got sued or charged with a crime. Ultimately, fake electors did meet on December 14th, 2020 in Arizona, Georgia, Michigan, Pennsylvania, New Mexico, Nevada, and Wisconsin. At the request of the Trump campaign, the electors from these battleground states signed documents falsely asserting that they were the quote, 'duly elected electors,' from their state and submitted them to the National Archives and to Vice President Pence in his capacity as President of the Senate. Here is what some of the fake electors' certificates look like as compared to the real ones. But these ballots had no legal effect. In an email produced to the Select Committee, Dr. Eastman told a Trump campaign representative that it did not matter that the electors had not been approved by a state authority.

"Quote, 'the fact that we have multiple slate of electors demonstrates the uncertainty of either. That should be enough'. He urged that Pence act boldly and be challenged. Documents produced to the Select Committee show that the Trump campaign took steps to ensure that the physical copies of the fake electors' electoral votes from two states were delivered to Washington for January 6th. Text messages exchanged between Republican Party officials in Wisconsin showed that on January 4th, the Trump campaign asked for someone to fly their fake electors' documents to Washington. A staffer for Wisconsin Senator Ron Johnson texted a staffer for Vice President Pence just minutes before the beginning of the joint session. This staffer stated that Senator Johnson wished to hand- deliver to the Vice President the fake electors' votes from Michigan and Wisconsin. The Vice President's aide unambiguously instructed them not to deliver the fake votes to the Vice President.

"Even though the fake electors' slates were transmitted to Congress and the executive branch, the Vice President held firm in his position that his role was to count lawfully submitted electoral votes."

Mike Pence: "Joseph Biden, Jr of the state of Delaware has received 306 votes. Donald J Trump of the state of Florida has received 232 votes."

Casey Lucier: "Which is what he did when the joint session resumed on January 6th after the attack on the Capitol."

Adam Schiff: "Well, we just heard in that video was an aide to the White House chief of staff telling this committee that the White House counsel's office felt that this fake electors plan was not legally sound. Nevertheless, the Trump campaign went forward with the scheme anyway. Speaker Bowers, were you aware that fake electors had met in Phoenix on December 14th and purported to cast electoral votes for President Trump?"

Rusty Bowers: "I was not."

Adam Schiff: "When you learned that these electors had met and sent their electoral votes to Washington, what did you think?"

Rusty Bowers: "Well, I thought of the book, The Gang That Couldn't Shoot Straight. And I just thought, this is a — this is a tragic parody."

Adam Schiff: "Mr. Bowers, I understand that as you flew from Phoenix to Washington yesterday, you reflected upon some passages from a personal journal that you were keeping in December 2020 while all of this was taking place. With your permission, I'm wondering if you would be willing to share one passage in particular with us."

Rusty Bowers: "Thank you very much. It is painful to have friends who have been such a help to me turn on me with such rancor. I may in the eyes of men not hold correct opinions or act according to their vision or convictions, but I do not take this current situation in a light manner, a fearful manner, or a vengeful manner. I do not want to be a winner by cheating. I will not play with laws I swore allegiance to. With any contrived desire towards deflection of my deep foundational desire to follow God's will as I believe He led my conscience to embrace. How else will I ever approach Him in the wilderness of life? Knowing that I ask this guidance only to show myself a coward in defending the course He let me take — He led me to take."

Adam Schiff: "Thank you, Mr. Speaker. Those are powerful words. I understand that taking the courageous positions that you did following the 2020 election in defense of the rule of law and protecting the voters of Arizona resulted in you and your family being subjected to protests and terrible threats. Can you tell us how this impacted you and your family?"

Rusty Bowers: "Well, as others in the videos have mentioned, we received, my secretaries would say, in excess of 20,000 emails and tens of thousands of voicemails and texts which saturated our offices. And we were unable to work, at least communicate, that at home, up till even recently, it is the new pattern or a pattern in our lives to worry what will happen on Saturdays because we have various groups come by and they have had video panel trucks with videos of me proclaiming me to be a pedophile and a pervert and a corrupt politician and blaring loudspeakers in my neighborhood and leaving literature both on my property, and — but arguing and threatening with neighbors and with myself.

"And I don't know if I should name groups, but there was a — one gentleman that had the three bars on his chest. And he had a pistol and was threatening my neighbor. Not with the pistol, but just vocally. When I saw the gun, I knew I had to get close. And at the same time, on some of these we had a daughter who is gravely ill, who is upset by what was happening outside. And my wife that is a valiant person, very, very strong, quiet, very strong woman. So it was disturbing. It was disturbing."

Adam Schiff: "Mr. Speaker, I want to thank you for your service to the state of Arizona and to the country. Mr. Chairman, at this point, I think it'd be appropriate to take a short recess. Accordingly. I reserve the balance of my time."

Bennie Thompson: "The Chair requests that those in the hearing room remain seated until the Capitol Police have escorted members and witnesses from the room. We'll have five minutes — five minute recess."

Bennie Thompson: "The committee will be in order. President Trump's pressure campaign against state officials existed in all the key battleground states that he lost, but the former president had a particular obsession with Georgia. Here is the president on the afternoon of January 6th after his own attorney general warned him that the claims you are about to hear are patently false."

[multimedia]

Donald Trump: "They should find those votes. They should absolutely find that. Just over 11,000 votes, that's all we need. They defrauded us out of a win in Georgia, and we're not going to forget it."

Bennie Thompson: "So, the state of Georgia is where we will turn our attention to next. I want to emphasize that our investigation into these issues is still ongoing. As I stated in our last hearing, if you have relevant information or documentary evidence to share with the select committee, we welcome your cooperation, but we will share some of our findings with you today.

"Secretary Raffensperger, thank you for being here today. You've been a public servant in Georgia since 2015, serving first as a member of the Georgia House of Representatives and then, since January 2019, as Georgia's Secretary of state. As a self-described conservative Republican, it is — is it fair to say that you wanted President Trump to win the 2020 election?"

Brad Raffensperger: "Yes, it is."

Bennie Thompson: "Mr. Secretary, many witnesses have told the Select Committee that Election Day, November 3rd, 2020, was a largely uneventful day in their home states. In spite of the challenges of conducting an election during a pandemic, you wrote in The Washington Post that the election was 'successful.' Tell us, what was your impression of how Election Day had proceeded in Georgia?"

Brad Raffensperger: "On Election Day in November, our election went remarkably smooth. In fact, we meet at the GEMA headquarters. That's the Georgia Energy — Emergency Management Association meeting location, but we were following wait times in line in the afternoon. Our average wait time was three minutes statewide that we were recording for various precincts, and it actually got down to two minutes.

"And at the end of the day, we felt that we had a successful election from the standpoint of the administration and the operation of the election."

Bennie Thompson: "Thank you. The chair recognizes the gentleman from California, Mr. Schiff."

Adam Schiff: "Thank you, Mr. Chairman. Secretary Raffensperger, did Joe Biden win the 2020 presidential election in Georgia, and by what margin?"

Brad Raffensperger: "President Biden carried the state of Georgia by approximately 12,000 votes."

Adam Schiff: "And Mr. Secretary, as I understand it, your office took several steps to ensure the accuracy of the vote count in Georgia, reviewing the vote count in at least three different ways. These steps included a machine recount, a forensic audit, and a full hand recount of every one of the five million ballots cast.

"Did these efforts, including a recount of literally every ballot cast in the state of Georgia, confirm the result?"

Brad Raffensperger: "Yes, they did. We counted the ballots with — the first tabulation would be scanned. Then when we did our 100 percent hand audit of the entire — all five million ballots in the state of Georgia, all cast in place, all absentee ballots, they were all hand recounted, and they came remarkably close to the first count.

"And then, upon the election being certified, President Trump, because he was in — within a half percent — excuse me — could ask for a recount, and then we recounted them again through the scanner, so we got remarkably the same count. Three counts, all remarkably close, which showed that President Trump did come up short."

Adam Schiff: "Nevertheless, as you will see, the president and his allies began in making — began making numerous false allegations of voter fraud, false allegations that you and Mr. Sterling, among others, had to address. Mr. Sterling, thank you also for being here today. Following the 2020 election, in addition to your normal duties, I understand that you became a spokesperson to try to combat disinformation about the election and the danger it was creating for elections officials, among others.

"In a December 1 press conference, you addressed some of your remarks directly to President Trump.

"Let's take a look at what you said that day."

> [multimedia]
> **Gabriel Sterling**: **"Mr. President, it looks like you likely lost the state of Georgia. We're investigating. There's always a possibility — I get it, and you have the rights to go to the courts. What you don't have the ability to do, and you need to step up and say this, is stop inspiring people to commit potential acts of violence.**
>
> **"Someone's going to get hurt, someone's going to get shot, someone's going to get killed, and it's not right. I — I — it's not right."**

Adam Schiff: "Mr. Sterling, what prompted you to make these remarks."

Gabriel Sterling: "Mr. Schiff, we had had a previously scheduled press conference that day, as we were in the habit of doing, trying to be as transparent as we could about the election and the counts going on. A little after lunch that day, lunchtime, I received a call from the project manager from Dominion Voting Systems, who was oddly audibly shaken.

"She's not the kind of person I would assume would be that way. She has a master's from MIT, a graduate of Naval Academy, and is very much on the ball and pretty unflappable. And she informed me about a — a young contractor they had who had been receiving threats from a — a video had been posted by some QAnon supporters.

"And at that point, we had been sort of — been steeping in this kind of stuff, so we were — it was around us all the time, so I — I didn't take note of it more than adding to the pile of other stuff we were having to deal with. And I did pull up Twitter and I scrolled through it, and I saw the young man's name.

"It was a particular tweet that, for lack of a better word, was the straw that broke the camel's back. Had the young man's name. It's a very unique name. I believed it was first generation American, and said – had his name, you committed treason, may God have mercy on your soul, with a slowly twisting gif of a noose.

"And for lack of a better word, I lost it. I just got irate. My boss was with me at the time, Deputy Secretary Jordan Fuchs, and she could tell that I was angry. I was turning — I tend to turn red from here up when that happens, and that happened at that time. And she called Secretary Raffensperger to say we're seeing these kind of threats, and Gabe thinks we need to say something about it. And Secretary said yes, and that's what prompted me to do what I did.

"I lost my temper, but it seemed necessary at the time because it was just getting worse. And I don't — I could not tell you why that particular one was the one that put me over the edge, but it did."

Adam Schiff: "Now, after you made this plea to the president, did Donald Trump urge his supporters to avoid the use of violence?"

Gabriel Sterling: "Not to my knowledge."

Adam Schiff: "Now, as we know, the president was aware of your speech because he tweeted about it later that day.

"Let's take a look at what the president said. In the tweet, Donald Trump claims that there was 'massive voter fraud in Georgia.' Mr. Sterling, that was just plain false, wasn't it?"

Gabriel Sterling: "Yes, sir."

Adam Schiff: "Nevertheless, the very next day, on December 2nd, President Trump released a lengthy video again making false claims of election fraud in Georgia. Let's take a look at what he said this time."

> **[multimedia]**
> **Donald Trump: "They found thousands and thousands of votes that were out of whack, all against me."**

Adam Schiff: "In fact, the day after Donald Trump released that video, so now we're talking just two days after the emotional warning that you gave that someone's going to get killed, representatives of President Trump appeared in Georgia, including Rudy Giuliani, and launched a new conspiracy theory that would take on a life of its own and threaten the lives of several innocent election workers.

"This story falsely alleges that sometime during election night, election workers at the State Farm Arena in Atlanta, Georgia kicked out poll observers. After the observers left, the story goes, these workers pulled so-called suitcases of ballots from under a table and ran those ballots through counting machines multiple times.

"Completely without evidence, President Trump and his allies claimed that these suitcases contained as many as 18,000 ballots, all for Joe Biden. None of this was true, but Rudy Giuliani appeared before the Georgia State Senate and played a surveillance video from State Farm Arena falsely claiming that it showed this conspiracy taking place.

"Here's a sample of what Mr. Giuliani had to say during that hearing."

[multimedia]
Rudy Giuliani: "And when you look at what you saw on the video, which to me was a smoking gun, powerful smoking gun, well, I don't — don't have to be a genius to figure out what happened. And I — I don't have to be a genius to figure out that those votes are not legitimate votes. You don't put legitimate votes under a table –"

Unknown: "No."

Rudy Giuliani: "Wait until you throw the opposition out and, in the middle of the night, count them. We would have to be fools to think that."

Adam Schiff: "President Trump's campaign amplified Giuliani's false testimony in a tweet, pushing out the video footage. Giuliani likewise pushed out his testimony on social media. As you can see in this tweet, Mr. Giuliani wrote that it was 'now beyond doubt' that Fulton County Democrats had stolen the election.

"Later in this hearing, we'll hear directly from one of the election workers in this video about the effect these lies had on her and on her family.

"Mr. Sterling, did the investigators in your office review the entire surveillance tape from the State Farm Arena on election night?"

Gabriel Sterling: "They actually reviewed approximately 48 hours going over the time period where — where action was taking place at the counting center at State Farm Arena."

Adam Schiff: "And what did the tape actually show?"

Gabriel Sterling: "Depending on which time you want to start, because as was mentioned this conspiracy theory took on a life of its own where they conflated a water main break that wasn't a water main break and throwing observers out and a series of other things. What it actually showed was Fulton County election workers engaging in normal ballot processing.

"One of the specific things — one of the things that was very frustrating was the so-called suitcases of ballots from under the table. If you watch the entirety of the video, you saw that these were election workers who were under the impression they were going to get to go home around 10, 10:30. People are putting on their coats.

"They're putting ballots that are prepared to be scanned into ballot carriers that are then sealed with tamper proof seals so that you — they can — you know they're not messed with. And the — it's an interesting thing cause you watch all — there's four screens of the video. And as you're watching it, you can see the election monitors in the corner with the press as they're taking these ballot carriers and putting them under the — under the table.

"You see it there. One of the other hidden ones, if you looked at the actual tape, was on the outside of the table. Just from the camera angle you couldn't see it originally. And this goes under the no good deed goes unpunished. "We were told — we were at GMA, as the Secretary pointed out. And we were under the — we were told that it looked like they were shutting down the Fulton County counting.

"The se — Secretary expressed some displeasure with that because we wanted to have everybody keep counting so we could get to the results and know what was happening. So our elections director called their elections director who was at another location, because this was Election Day. There was two different places where ballot things were being done by the Fulton County office.

"So he called — the elections director for Fulton then called Ralph Jones, who was at the State Farm Arena and said what the heck are you doing? Go ahead and stay. And as you watch the video itself, you see him take the phone call as people are putting things away and getting ready to leave. And you can tell for about 15, 20 seconds, he does not want to tell these people they have to stay.

"He walks over, he thinks about it for a second. You see him come back to the corner of a desk and kind of slumps his shoulders and says Ok, y'all, we got to keep on counting. And then you see them take their coats off, get the ballots out. And then a secondary thing that you'll see on there is you'll have people who are counting ballots who a batch will go through, they will take them off and run that through again.

"What happens there is a standard operating procedure. That if there is a missed scan, if there's a misalignment, if it doesn't read right — these are high speed, high capacity scanners. So three or four will go through after a mis-scan. You have to delete that batch and put it back through again. And by going through the hand tally, as the Secretary pointed out, we showed that if there had been multiple ballots scanned without a, you know, corresponding physical ballot, your counts would have been a lot higher than the ballots themselves.

"And by doing the hand tally, we saw two specific numbers that were me — met. The hand tally got us to a .1053 percent off of the total votes cast and .0099 percent on the margin, which is essentially dead on accurate. Most academic studies say on a hand tally you will have between one and two percent. But because we use ballot marking devices where it's very clear what the voter intended, it made it a lot easier to us — for us to conduct that hand count and show that none of that was true."

Adam Schiff: "Now I understand that when you reviewed these tapes and did the analysis, it disproved this con – conspiracy theory. But you still had to take a lot of steps to try to make sure the public knew the truth about these allegations. And you did frequent briefings for the press. Let's take a look at one of those press briefings, Mr. Sterling, that you held on December 7th to make the point that you just did today."

[multimedia]

Gabriel Sterling: "Move on to what I'm going to call disinformation Monday. Out of the gate, many of you all saw the videotape from State Farm Arena. I spent hours with our post certified investigators. Justin Gray from WSB spent hours with us going over this video to explain to people that what you saw, the secret suitcases of magic ballots, were actually ballots that had been packed into those absentee ballot carriers by the workers in plain view of the monitors and the press.

"And what's really frustrating is the President's attorneys had this same videotape. They saw the exact same things the rest of us could see. And they chose to mislead state Senators and the public about what was on that video. I'm quite sure that they will not characterize the video if they try to enter into evidence because that is the kind of thing that can lead to sanctions because it's obviously untrue.

"They knew it was untrue and they continue to do things like this."

<u>**Adam Schiff**</u>: "Mr. Sterling, despite the efforts by your office to combat this misinformation — misinformation by speaking out publicly and through local media, you were unable to match the reach of President Trump's platform and social media megaphone spreading these false conspiracy theories. What was it like to compete with the President, who had the biggest bully pulpit in the world to push out these false claims?"

<u>**Gabriel Sterling**</u>: "For lack of a better word, it was frustrating. But oftentimes I felt our information was getting out, but that there was a reticence of people who needed to believe it to believe it because the President of the United States, who many looked up to and respected, was telling them it wasn't true despite the facts.

"And I have characterized at one point it was kind of like a shovel trying to empty the ocean. And yes, it was frustrating. I even have, you know, family members who I had to argue with about some of these things. And I would show them things. And the problem you have is you're getting to people's hearts.

"I remember there's one specific — an attorney that we know that we showed him, walked him through.

"This wasn't true. Ok, I get that. This wasn't true. Ok, I get that. This wasn't — five or six things. But at the end he goes, I just know in my heart they cheated. That's the stan — and so once you get past the heart, the facts don't matter as much.

"And our job from our point of view was to get the facts out, do our job, tell the truth, follow the Constitution, follow the law, and defend the institutions. And the institutions held."

Adam Schiff: "Let's take a look at what you were competing with. This is former — the former President speaking in Georgia on December 5th."

> **[multimedia]**
> **Donald Trump: "But it's a fraud. It's overwhelming. And again, I'm going to ask you to look up at that very, very powerful and very expensive screen. [multimedia]"**
>
> **Unknown: "Hidden cases of possible ballots are rolled out from under a table. Four people under a cloud of suspicion."**
>
> **Donald Trump: "So if you just take the crime of what those Democrats — workers were doing — and by the way there was no water main break. You know, they said there — there was no water main break. That's 10 times more than I need to win this state. 10 times more. That's 10 times, maybe more than that, but it's 10 times more because we lost by a very close number."**

Adam Schiff: "In this committee's hearing last Monday, we heard from senior federal law enforcement officials – from the senior most federal law enforcement official in

Atlanta at the time, US Attorney for the Northern District BJay Pak, as well as former Attorney General Bill Barr. They both testified that the allegations were thoroughly investigated and found to have no merit.

"Here is US Attorney Pak."

> **[multimedia]**
> **BJay Pak: "In particular to Attorney General Barr, I told him that we looked into it. We've done several things including interviewing the witnesses. I listened to the — the tapes and reviewed the videotape myself and that there was nothing there. Giuliani was wrong in representing that this was a suitcase full of ballots."**

Adam Schiff: "And here's what Attorney General Bill Barr had to say about the same allegations."

> **[multimedia]**
> **William Barr: "Took a look — hard look at this ourselves. And based on our review of and including the interviews of the key witnesses, the Fulton County allegations were — had no merit."**

Adam Schiff: "We also have testimony from senior Department of Justice officials establishing that they specifically told President Trump that these allegations had been thoroughly investigated and were completely without merit.

"Here is Acting Attorney — Deputy Attorney General Richard Donoghue describing a phone conversation in which he specifically told President Trump that these allegations were false."

> **[multimedia]**

Richard Donoghue: "They kept fixating on this suitcase that supposedly had fraudulent ballots in it. The suitcase was rolled out from under the table. And I said no, Sir. There is no suitcase. You can watch that video over and over. There is no suitcase. There is a wheeled bin where they ca –"

Adam Schiff: "Where they carry the ballots. No matter how many times Senior Department of Justice officials, including his own Attorney General, told the President that these allegations were not true, President Trump kept promoting these lies and putting pressure on state officials to accept them. On January 2nd, the President had a lengthy telephone conversation with Secretary Raffensperger.

"Prior to the President's call, though, I want to share a bit of important context. First, the White House, including the former President's Chief of Staff Mark Meadows repeatedly called or texted the Secretary's office some 18 times in order to set up this call.

"They were quite persistent. Second, Chief of Staff Mark Meadows took the extraordinary step of showing up at a signature audit site in Georgia where he met with Secretary Raffensperger's chief investigator Frances Watson who was supervising that audit process. Behind me is a photograph from that visit. Third, the day after Meadows' Georgia visit, he set up a call between President Trump and Frances Watson.

"On the call between President Trump and Georgia investigator Frances Watson, the former President continued to push the false claim that he'd won the state of Georgia. Let's listen to that part of the conversation."

[multimedia]

Donald Trump: "You know, it's just you have the most important job in the country right now. Because if we win Georgia — first of all if we win you're gonna have two wins. Well you're not — they're not going to win right now. You know, they're down because the people of Georgia are so angry at what happened to me. They know I won.

"Won by hundreds of thousands of votes. It wasn't close."

Adam Schiff: "And in this next clip, he told this state law enforcement official that she'd be praised if she found the right answer."

[multimedia]
Donald Trump: "Hopefully, you know, I will — when — when the right answer comes out you'll be praised. I mean, I don't know why, you know, they made it so hard. And you — they will be praised. People will say great.

"Because that's what it's about, that ability to check and to — and to make it right. Because everyone knows it's wrong.

"There's just no way."

Adam Schiff: "Mr. Raffensperger, I know you weren't on this call, but — but that you have listened to it. President Trump didn't win by hundreds of thousands of votes in Georgia, did he?"

Brad Raffensperger: "No, he did not. I've been traveling through the state of Georgia for a year now and simply put in a nutshell, what happened in fall of 2020 is that 28,000 Georgians skipped the Presidential race and yet they voted down ballot in other races. And the Republican

Congressman ended up getting 33,000 more votes than President Trump.

"And that's why President Trump came up short."

Adam Schiff: "Thank you, Mr. Secretary. The President on this call doesn't stop here. Let's listen to another part of the conversation between President Trump and Ms. Watson."

> **[multimedia]**
> **Donald Trump: "Anyway, but whatever you can do, Frances, it would be — it's a great thing. It's an important thing for the country. So important. You have no idea, it's so important –"**
>
> **Frances Watson: "– Well, Mr. –"**
>
> **Donald Trump: "– And I very much appreciate it."**

Adam Schiff: "Whatever you can do, Frances. This is the President of the United States calling an investigator looking into the election in which he is a candidate and asking her to do whatever you can do. Mr. Secretary, he placed this call to your chief investigator on September 23rd, 2020. The subcommittee has received text messages indicating that Mark Meadows wanted to send some of the investigators in her office in the words of one White House aide a shitload of POTUS stuff, including coins, actual autographed MAGA hats, etc.

"White House staff intervened to make sure that didn't happen. It was clear at the time of this call that the former President had his sights set on January 6th. Listen to this portion when he told Frances Watson about a very important date."

[multimedia]
Donald Trump: "Do you think you'll be
Working after Christmas to keep it going fast?
Because, you know, we have that date of the
6th, which is a very important date."

Adam Schiff: "That important date, of course, was the
joint session of Congress where Georgia's electoral votes
would be counted for Joe Biden. A little — a little over a
week after this call to Frances Watson, the President was
finally able to speak with you, Secretary Raffensperger.
Bear in mind as we discussed this call today that by this
point in time, early January, the election in Georgia had
already been certified.

"But perhaps more important, the President of the United
States had already been told repeatedly by his own top
Justice Department officials that the claims he was about
to make to you about massive fraud in Georgia were
completely false.

"Mr. Secretary, the call between you and the President
lasted 67 minutes, over an hour. We obviously can't listen
to the entire recording here today, although it is available
on the Select Committee's website. But we'll listen to
selected excerpts of it now so that we can get your
insights. Let's begin with the President raising the
thoroughly debunked allegations of suitcases of ballots."

[multimedia]
Donald Trump: "Weren't in an official voter
box. They were in what looked to be suitcases
or trunks. Suitcases, but they weren't in — in
voter boxes."

Donald Trump: "The minimum number it
could be — because we watched it and they —
they watched it and certified in slow motion,
instant replay, if you can believe it, but it had

slow motion and it was magnified many times over. And the minimum it was was 18,000 ballots, all for Biden."

Adam Schiff: "These are the allegations that the Department of Justice, the attorney general, the Georgia Bureau of Investigation, and your office had all said were false. Is that right?"

Brad Raffensperger: "Correct. And even more importantly, when BJ Pak resigned as US attorney of the Northern District, President Trump appointed as acting US attorney of the Northern District Bobby Christine. And Bobby Christine looked at that and he was quoted the AJC [ph] that he found nothing, and he dismissed that case early also."

Adam Schiff: "Thank you, Mr. Secretary. The President references suitcases or trunks. Mr. Sterling, were the objects seen in these videos suitcases or trunks or were they just the ordinary containers that are used by election workers?"

Gabriel Sterling: "They're stand — standard ballot carriers that allow for seals to be put on them so that they are tamper proof."

Adam Schiff: "And finally, the President claims that there was a minimum of 18,000 ballots somehow smuggled in all for Biden. I take it, gentlemen, that was also categorically false?"

Gabriel Sterling: "There's no — A, there's no physical way he can know who those ballots were for. But secondarily, we had — Fulton County for years, has been an issue in our state when it comes to elections. So we had a — they had a very difficult time during the primary — in large part because of COVID. So we had put them under a consent decree the secretary got negotiated where we had a monitor on site and his name was Carter Jones.

"And he took a notation. He had gone from State Farm to the English Street warehouse to look at Election Day activities. But before he left the State Farm arena, he noted how many ballots have been counted on each one of the machines. And when he came back after we found out they were working again, he took note again when they closed.

"And I believe the final number was something around 8,900 total ballots were scanned from the time he left to the time about 12:30 or 1:00 in the morning. So way below 18,000."

Adam Schiff: "Let's play the next clip."

> **[multimedia]**
> **Donald Trump: "I heard it was close, so I said there's no way. But they dropped a lot of votes in their late at night. You know that, Brad."**

Adam Schiff: "Mr. Secretary, did somebody drop — drop a lot of votes there late at night?"

Brad Raffensperger: "No, I believe that the President was referring to some of the counties when they would upload, but the ballots had all been accepted and had to be accepted by state law by 7 pm. So there were no additional ballots accepted after 7 pm."

Adam Schiff: "Let's play the next clip in which the President makes claims about so-called dead voters."

> **[multimedia]**
> **Donald Trump: "The other thing, dead people. So dead people voted. And I think the — the number is in the close to 5,000 people. And they went to obituaries. They went to all sorts**

**of methods to come up with an accurate
number. And a minimum is close to about
5,000 voters."**

Adam Schiff: "So Secretary, did your office investigated whether those allegations were accurate? Did 5,000 dead people in Georgia vote?"

Brad Raffensperger: "No, it's not accurate. And actually in their lawsuits they allege 10,315 dead people. We found two dead people when I wrote my letter to Congress that's dated January six, and subsequent to that we found two more. That's one, two, three, four people. Not 4,000, but just a total four. Not 10,000. Not 5,000."

Adam Schiff: "Let's play the next clip."

[multimedia]
**Donald Trump: "And there's nothing wrong
with saying that, you know, that you've
recalculated because it's 2,236 in absentee
ballots. I mean, they're all exact numbers that
were — were done by accounting firms, law
firms, etc. And even if you cut them in half, cut
them in half, and cut them in half. Again, it's
more votes than we need."**

Adam Schiff: "Mr. Secretary, is there any way that you could have lawfully changed the result in the state of Georgia and somehow explained it away as a recalculation?"

Brad Raffensperger: "No, the numbers are the numbers. The numbers don't lie. We had many allegations and we investigated every single one of them. In fact, I challenged my team, did we miss anything?

"They said that there was over 66,000 underage voters. We found that there was actually zero. You can register to vote in Georgia when you're 17 and a half.

"You have to be 18 by Election Day. We checked that out. Every single voter. They said that there was 2,423 nonregistered voters. There were zero. They said that there was 2,056 felons. We identified less than 74 or less that were actually still on a felony sentence. Every single allegation we checked, we ran down the rabbit trail to make sure that our numbers were accurate."

Adam Schiff: "So there's no way you could have recalculated it, except by fudging the numbers?"

Brad Raffensperger: "The numbers were the numbers and we could not recalculate because we had made sure that we had checked every single allegation. And we had many investigations; we had nearly thrown from the 2020 election."

Adam Schiff: "Mr. Secretary, you tried to push back when the President made these unsupported claims, whether they were about suitcases of ballots or that Biden votes were counted three times. Let's play the next clip."

> **[multimedia]**
> **Brad Raffensperger: "Mr. President, they did not put that plea. We — we — we did an audit of that and we proved conclusively that they were not scanned three times. Yes, Mr. President, we'll send you the link from WSB –"**
>
> **Donald Trump: "I don't care about a link. I don't need it. I have a much better — we're gonna have a much better link."**

Adam Schiff: "You told the President you would send him a link from WSB, which I understand is a local television station that had a unedited video from the State Farm Arena. But the President wasn't interested in that. He said he had a much better link. Mr. Secretary, at the time that you were on the call with the President as we have shown both the FBI and the Georgia Bureau of Investigation had proven these claims to be nonsense.

"And you told him about these investigations on the phone. Let's listen to what President Trump had to say about the state and federal law enforcement officers who conducted, who investigated these false claims."

> **[multimedia]**
> **Donald Trump: "There's no way they could —
> then they're incompetent. They're either
> dishonest –"**
>
> **Cleta Mitchell: "Well, what did they find?"**
>
> **Donald Trump: "Then there's only two
> answers. Dishonesty or incompetence. There's
> just no way. Look, there's no way."**

Adam Schiff: "But the President didn't stop at insinuating that law enforcement officers were either dishonest or incompetent. He went on to suggest that you could be subject to criminal liability for your role in the matter. Before I play that portion of the conversation, I'd like to show you something that the President retweeted a couple of weeks before your call with him.

"Here's the President retweeting a post from one of his allies, a lawyer, who was later sanctioned by a judge in Michigan for making false claims of election fraud. Let's take a look at that tweet. The tweet read quote, 'President Trump @realDonaldTrump is a genuinely good man. He does not really like to fire people.

"I bet he dislikes putting people in jail, especially 'Republicans'. He gave @BrianKempGA & @GASecofState every chance to get it right. They refused. They will soon be going to jail.' So on your call, this was not the first time the President was suggesting you might be criminally liable. With that, let's listen to this portion of the call."

[multimedia]

<u>Donald Trump</u>: "I think you're going to find that they are shredding ballots because they have to get rid of the ballots because the ballots are unsigned, the ballots are — are corrupt and they're brand new and they don't have seals and there's a whole thing with the ballots, but the ballots are corrupt and you're going to find that they are — which is totally illegal.

"It's — it's more illegal for you than it is for them. Because you know what they did and you're not reporting it. That's a — you know, that's a criminal — that's a criminal offense. And you know, you can't let that happen. That's — that's a big risk to you and to Ryan, your lawyer. And that's a big risk."

<u>Adam Schiff</u>: "Secretary Raffensperger, after making a false claim about shredding of ballots, the President suggested that you may be committing a crime by not going along with his claims of election fraud.

"And after suggesting that you might have criminal exposure, President Trump makes his most explicit ask of the call.

"Let's play a part of that conversation."

[multimedia]

Donald Trump: "So, look, all I want to do is this. I just want to find 11,780 votes, which is one more than we have because we won the state."

Adam Schiff: "Mr. Secretary, was the President here asking you for exactly what he wanted? One more vote than his opponent."

Brad Raffensperger: "What I knew is that we didn't have any votes to find. We had continued to look. We investigated. I could have shared the numbers with you. There were no votes to find. That was an accurate count that had been certified. And as our general counsel said, there was no shredding of ballots."

Adam Schiff: "Mr. Secretary, after making this request the President then goes back to the danger of having you deny these allegations of fraud. Let's listen to that part of the clip."

[multimedia]
Donald Trump: "And I watched you this morning and you said well, there was no criminality, but I mean, all of this stuff is — is very dangerous stuff. When you talk about no criminality, I think it's very dangerous for you to say that."

Adam Schiff: "Secretary Raffensperger, you wrote about this in your book and you said, quote, 'I felt then and still believe today that this was a threat'. Others obviously thought so too because some of Trump's more radical followers have responded as if it was their duty to carry out this threat. Please tell us what you or your wife, even your daughter in law experienced regarding threats from Trump's more radical followers."

Brad Raffensperger: "Well, after the — after the election, my email, my cell phone was docked. And so I was getting texts all over the country. And then eventually my wife started getting the text and hers typically came in a sexualized attacks which were disgusting. You have to understand that Trish and I, we met in high school.

"We've married over 40 years now. And so they started going after her I think just to probably put pressure on me. Why don't you just quit walk away. And so that happened. And then some people broke into my daughter in law's home and my son has passed and she's widow and has two kids. And so we're very concerned about her safety also."

Adam Schiff: "And Mr. Secretary, why didn't you just quit and walk away?"

Brad Raffensperger: "Because I knew that we had followed the law, we had followed the Constitution And I think sometimes moments require you to stand up and just take the shots. You're doing your job. And that's all we did. You know, we just followed the law and we followed the Constitution. And at the end of the day, President Trump came up short.

"But I had to be faithful to the Constitution. And that's what I swore an oath to do."

Adam Schiff: "During the remainder of the call, the former President continued to press you to find the remaining votes that would ensure his victory in Georgia. Let's listen to a little more."

> **[multimedia]**
> **Donald Trump: "Why wouldn't you want to find the right answer, Brad, instead of keep saying that the numbers are right? So look, can you get together tomorrow? And Brad, we just want the truth. It's simple. And – and**

everyone's going to look very good if the truth comes out. It's Ok. It takes a little while, but let the truth come out.

"And the truth — the real truth is I won by 400,000 votes, at least. So — so what are we going to do here? Because I only need 11,000 votes. Fellas, I need 11,000 votes. Give me a break."

Adam Schiff: "Four days after the President's call to Secretary Raffensperger was January 6th. The President whipped up the crowd in front of the Ellipse, once again promoting the allegation that Secretary Raffensperger, the President's own attorney general, had told him was false. Here he is on the Ellipse."

[multimedia]
Donald Trump: "In Fulton County, Republican poll watchers were rejected in some cases physically from the room under the false pretense of a pipe burst — water main burst. Everybody leave. Which we now know was a total lie. Then election officials pulled boxes, Democrats, and suitcases of ballots out from under a table, you all it saw on television, totally fraudulent, and illegally scanned them for nearly two hours, totally unsupervised.

"Tens of thousands of votes. This act coincided with a mysterious vote dump of up to 100,000 votes for Joe Biden, almost none for Trump. Oh, that sounds fair. That was at 1:34 am."

Adam Schiff: "Mr. Secretary, Mr. Sterling, I want to thank you for your service to the state of Georgia and to the country. Speaker Bowers, likewise, I want to thank you for your service to the State of Arizona and to the country.

You have served not only your home states, but our nation and our democracy. Mr. Chairman, I yield back."

Bennie Thompson: "Thank you, Mr. Schiff. I thank the witnesses for joining us today. You are now dismissed."

[Panel Switches]

"I now welcome to our final witness this afternoon, Wandrea 'Shaye' Moss. Ms. Moss worked in the Department of Registration and Elections in Fulton County, Georgia from 2017 until 2022. In that job, Ms. Moss handled voter applications and absentee ballot requests, and also helped to process the vote count for several elections.

"In December 2020, Ms. Moss and her mother, Ms. Ruby Freeman, became the target of nasty lies spread by President Trump and his allies as they sought to overturn the election results in Georgia.

"Ms. Moss and her mother, Ms. Freeman, are two of the unsung heroes in this country doing the hard work of keeping our democracy functioning for every American.

"Ms. Moss, welcome. Thank you for your service, and I thank you for being here today. I will now swear you in. Please stand. Do you swear or affirm under penalty of perjury that the testimony you're about to give is the truth, the whole truth, and nothing but the truth, so help you God?"

Shaye Moss: [Off mic]

Bennie Thompson: "Thank you. Please be seated. Let the record reflect that the witness answered in the affirmative. Ms. – Ms. Moss, thank you very much for being here today. I understand that you are here along with your mother today. Would you like to introduce your mom?"

Shaye Moss: [Off mic]

Bennie Thompson: "Ms. Moss, today we'll be asking you about some of the threats that you received following the 2020 election. Since you've been an election worker for over ten years, I want to ask you, in your decade of service, had you ever experienced threats like these before?"

Shaye Moss: [Off mic]

Bennie Thompson: "Don't be nervous, just — I understand. So — and I want to make sure that the record reflects that you've done it for quite a while and you've never received a threat, and your answer was no.

"Thank you. Pursuant to Section 5C8 of the House Resolution 503, the chair recognizes the gentleman from California, Mr. Schiff, for questions."

Adam Schiff: "Good afternoon, Ms. Moss. Thank you for being here. I understand that you were employed by the Fulton County Registration and Elections Department for more than ten years, and I understand that you loved that job. Please tell us what made you so fond of the work that you did."

Shaye Moss: "Well, I've always been told by my grandmother how important it is to vote and how people before me, a lot of people, older people in my family, did not have that right. So, what I loved most about my job were the older voters. Younger people could usually do everything from their phone or go online. But the older voters liked to call.

"They liked to talk to you. They like to get in my card. They liked to know that every election I'm here. And like even college students, a lot of parents trust in me to make sure their child does not have to drive home. They'll get an absentee ballot. They can vote. And I really found pleasure in that. I liked being the one that, you know, if someone can't navigate my voter page or, you know, they want a new precinct card, they don't have a copy machine or computer or all of that, I can put it in the mail for them.

"I was excited always about sending out all the absentee ballots for the elderly, disabled people. I even remember driving to a hospital to give someone her absentee application. That's — that's what I loved the most."

Adam Schiff: "So, you really enjoyed helping people vote and participate, and — and that was something, the right to vote, that your grandmother taught you was precious."

Shaye Moss: "Yes."

Adam Schiff: "Well, I know the events that we're here to talk about today are incredibly difficult to relive. Your proud service as an election worker took a dramatic turn on the day that Rudy Giuliani publicized the video of you and your mother counting ballots on election night. President Trump, Rudy Giuliani, and others claimed on the basis of this video that you and your mother were somehow involved in a plot to kick out observers, bring suitcases of false ballots for Biden into the arena, and then run them through the machines multiple times. None of that was true, was it?"

Shaye Moss: "None of it."

Adam Schiff: "I'd like to show you some of the statements that Rudy Giuliani made in a second hearing before the Georgia state legislator a week after that video clip from State Farm Arena was first circulated by Mr. Giuliani and President Trump. I want to advise viewers that these statements are completely false and also deeply disturbing."

[multimedia]

Rudy Giuliani: "Tape earlier in the day of Ruby Freeman and SHAYE Freeman Moss and one other gentleman quite obviously surreptitiously passing around USB ports as if they are vials of heroin or cocaine. I mean, it's our — it's obvious to anyone who's a criminal investigator or prosecutor they are engaged in surreptitious illegal activity again that day, and that's a week ago, and they're still walking around Georgia lying.

"They should have been — they should have been — should have been questioned already. Their places of work, their homes, should have been searched for evidence of ballots, for Ellis — evidence of USB ports, for evidence of voter fraud."

Adam Schiff: "That video was from Rudy Giuliani's appearance at a Georgia State Senate hearing on December 10.

"How did you become aware — how did you first become aware that Rudy Giuliani, the president's lawyer, was accusing you and your mother of a crime?"

Shaye Moss: "I was at work like always, and the former chief, Mr. Jones, asked me to come to his office. And when I went to his office, the former director, Ms. Varon [Ph], was in there, and they showed me a video on their computer. It was just like a very short clip of us working at State Farm, and it had someone on the video, like, talking over the video, just saying that we were doing things that we weren't supposed to do, just lying throughout the video.

"And that's when I first found out about it."

Adam Schiff: "And were there social media posts that they showed you responding to those false claims?"

Shaye Moss: "Well, when — when I saw the video, of course the first thing that I saw it was, like, why? What — why is — why are they doing this? What's going on? And they, you know, just told me that Trump and his allies were not satisfied with the outcome of the election, and they — they were getting a lot of threats and being harassed online and asked me, you know, have I been receiving anything, and I need to check on my mom.

"And I told them I — you know, I was, like, where? Where have they — you know, where have you been getting these threats? I — I don't believe I have any. And Mr. Jones told me, like, they're attacking his Facebook. And I don't really use Facebook. I have one so I went to the Facebook app. And I'm just kind of panicky at this point because this has never happened to me, and my mom is involved.

"I'm, like, her only child. So, I'm just — asked him, like, where are the messages? All I see is the feeds.

"Like, how do you get to the messages? And he said it's another icon on your phone that says Messenger. And I went to that icon, and it was just a lot of horrible things there."

Adam Schiff: "And those horrible things, did they include threats?"

Shaye Moss: "Yes, a lot of threats wishing death upon me, telling me that, you know, I'm — I'll be in jail with my mother, and saying things like be glad it's 2020 and not 1920, yes."

Adam Schiff: "Were — were a lot of these threats and — and vile comments racist in nature?"

Shaye Moss: "A lot of them were racist, a lot of them were just hateful, yes, sir."

Adam Schiff: "In one of the videos we just watched, Mr. Giuliani accused you and your mother of passing some sort of USB drive to each other. What was your mom actually handing you on that video?"

Shaye Moss: "A ginger mint."

Adam Schiff: "It wasn't just Rudy Giuliani. We heard President Trump make these false allegations repeatedly during his call with Secretary Raffensperger. Let's listen to a portion of what he had to say about you and your mother."

> **[multimedia]**
> **Donald Trump: "We had at least 18,000. That's on tape. We had them counted very painstakingly, 18,000 voters having to do with the Ruby Freeman. That's — she's a vote scammer, a professional vote scammer and hustler."**

Adam Schiff: "Donald Trump attacked you and your mother, using her name 18 times on that call, 18 times. Ms. Moss, can you describe what you experienced listening to former President Trump attack you and your mother in a call with the Georgia Secretary of State?"

Shaye Moss: "I felt horrible. I felt like it was all my fault, like if I would have never decided to be an elections worker, like, I could have — like, anything else, but that's what I decided to do. And now people are lying and spreading rumors and lies and attacking my mom, I'm her only child, going to my grandmother's house.

"I'm her only grandchild. And — and my kid is just — I felt so bad. I — I just felt bad for my mom, and I felt horrible for picking this job and being the one that always wants to help and always there, never missing not one election. I just felt like it was — it was my fault for putting my family in this situation."

Adam Schiff: "Well, it — it wasn't your fault. Your mother was kind enough to come speak with us earlier. Let's listen to her story in her words."

[multimedia]

Ruby Freeman: "My name is Ruby Freeman. I've always believed it when God says that he'll make your name great, but this is not the way it was supposed to be. I could have never imagined the events that followed the presidential election 2020. For my entire professional life, I was Lady Ruby. My community in Georgia where I was born and lived my whole life knew me as Lady Ruby.

"I built my own business around that name, LaRuby's Unique Treasures, a pop up shop catering to ladies with unique fashions. I wore a shirt that proudly proclaimed that I was and I am Lady Ruby.

"Actually, I had that shirt on — I had that shirt in every color. I wore that shirt on Election Day 2020. I haven't worn it since, and I'll never wear it again.

"Now I won't even introduce myself by my name anymore. I get nervous when I bump into someone I know in the grocery store who says my name. I'm worried about who's listening. I get nervous when I have to give my

name for food orders. I'm always concerned of who's around me. I've lost my name, and I've lost my reputation."

Ruby Freeman: "I've lost my sense of security, all because a group of people, starting with number 45 and his ally Rudy Giuliani, decided to scapegoat me and my daughter Shea to push their own lies about how the presidential election was stolen."

Adam Schiff: "Ms. Moss, how has this experience of being targeted by the former president and his allies affected your life?"

Shaye Moss: "This turned my life upside down. I no longer give out my business card. I don't transfer calls. I — I don't want anyone knowing my name. I don't want to go anywhere with my mom because she might yell my name out over the grocery aisle or something. I don't go to the grocery store at all. I haven't been anywhere at all.

"I've gained about 60 pounds. I just don't do nothing anymore. I don't want to go anywhere. I second guess everything that I do. It's affected my life in a — in a major way. In every way. All because of lies. For me doing my job, same thing I've been doing forever."

Adam Schiff: "Your mother also told this committee about how she had to leave her own home for her safety and go into hiding after the FBI told her that it would not be safe for her there before January 6th and until the inauguration. Let's listen to a clip of her story in her own words."

[multimedia]
Ruby Freeman: "Around the week of January 6th, the FBI informed me that I needed to

leave my home for safety. And I left my home for safety around that time."

Unknown: "Understood. How — how long did you stay out, did you, you know, remain outside of your home for your own safety?"

Ruby Freeman: "I — I stayed away from my home for approximately two months. It was horrible. I felt homeless. I felt, you know, I can't believe — I can't believe this person has caused this much damage to me and my family. To have to leave my home that I've lived there for 21 years. And, you know, I'm having to have my neighbors watch out for me. You know, and I have to go and stay with somebody.

"It was hard. It was horrible."

Unknown: "And the — your conversation with the FBI about needing to leave your home for your — your own safety or perhaps recommending it. Do you remember was there a specific threat that prompted that or was it the accumulation of — of threats that you had received?"

Ruby Freeman: "What prompted it was — was getting ready to — January 6th was about to come. And they did not want me to be at home because of all the threats and everything that I had gotten. They didn't want me to be there in fear of, you know, that people were coming to my home. And I had a lot of that, so they didn't want me to be there just in case something happened.

"I asked how long am I gonna have to be gone? They said at least until the inauguration."

Adam Schiff: "Ms. Moss, I understand that people once showed up at your grandmother's house. Tell us about that experience."

Shaye Moss: "I received a call from my grandmother. This woman is my everything. I've never even heard her or seen her cry ever in my life. And she called me screaming at the top of her lungs, like, 'Shaye, Shaye, oh my gosh, Shaye.' Just freaking me out saying that there are people at her home and they, you know, they knocked on the door and of course she opened it seeing who was there, who it was.

"And they just started pushing their way through, claiming that they were coming in to make a citizen's arrest. They needed to find me and my mom. They knew we were there. And she was just, like, screaming and didn't know what to do. And I wasn't there. So, you know, I just felt so helpless and so horrible for her.

"And she was just screaming. I told her to close the door. Don't open the door for — for anyone. And, you know, she's a 70 something I won't say year old woman. And she — she doesn't like having restrictions. She wants to answer the door. She likes to get her steps in walking around the neighborhood. And I had to tell her, like, you can't do that.

"You — you have to be safe. You know, she would tell me that at night people would just continuously send pizzas over and over to her home. You know, and they was expecting her to pay for these large amounts of pizzas. And she went through a lot that she didn't have to. And once again it made me just feel so horrible."

Adam Schiff: "In addition to the personal impact this experience has had on you and your family, one of the things that I find most disturbing is how these lies discourage longtime election workers from continuing to do this important work. Tell us if you would, of the other election workers shown in that State Farm Arena video and their supervisors, how many are still election workers in Fulton County?"

Shaye Moss: "There is no permanent election worker or supervisor in that video that's still there."

Adam Schiff: "And did you end up leading your — leaving your position as well?"

Shaye Moss: "Yes, I — I left."

Adam Schiff: "Ms. Moss, I want to thank you for coming in to speak with us and I thank you for your service to our democracy. What we have just played is a truly horrible and appalling sample, but just a sample of the things that were said about you and your mother following the election. I want to say how very sorry I think we all are for what you've gone through.

"And tragically you're not alone. Other election workers around the country have also been the subject of lies and threats. No election workers should be subject to such heinous treatment just for doing their job. With your permission, I would like to give your mother the last word."

Shaye Moss: "Yes."

Adam Schiff: "We're just going to play the tape."

> [multimedia]
> **Ruby Freeman: "There is nowhere I feel safe.**
> **Nowhere. Do you know how it feels to have the**
> **President of the United States to target you?**
> **The President of the United States is supposed**

to represent every American, not to target one. But he targeted me, Lady Rudy, a small business owner, a mother, a proud American citizen who stand up to help Fulton County run an election in the middle of the pandemic."

Adam Schiff: "Thank you, Ms. Moss. Thank you, Ms. Freeman, or as America now knows her, Lady Ruby, for your service to Fulton County, Georgia, our country, and our democracy. Mr. Chairman, I yield back."

Bennie Thompson: "Thank you, Mr. Schiff. Ms. Moss?"

Shaye Moss: "Yes, Sir."

Bennie Thompson: "I want to thank you for sharing with us the very troubling story of what you and your mother experienced. The harassment of election workers like you simply for doing your duty as public servants poses a threat to our democratic process. Your testimony is an important contribution to the work of our committee and serves as a reminder to all of us that the safety of local election officials is vital to ensuring that our elections are always free and fair.

"I want to thank our witness for joining us today. The members of the select committee may have additional questions for today's witness and we ask that you respond expeditiously in writing to those questions. Without objection, members will be permitted 10 business days to submit statements for the record, including opening remarks and additional questions for the witness.

"Without objection, the Chair recognizes the gentleman from California, Mr. Schiff , for a closing statement."

Adam Schiff: "For more than 200 years, our democracy has been distinguished by the peaceful transfer of power. When an American raises their right hand and takes the

Presidential oath of office, they are transformed from an ordinary citizen into the most powerful person in the world, the President. This is an awesome pire — power to acquire.

"It is even more awesome when is handed on peacefully. When George Washington relinquished the Office of the Presidency, it set a precedent that served as a beacon for other nations struggling against tyranny. When Ronald Reagan described it as a kind of miracle in the eyes of the world he was exactly right.

"Other countries use violence to seize and hold power, but not in the United States, not in America. When Donald Trump used the power of the Presidency to try to stay in office after losing the election to Joe Biden, he broke that sacred and centuries old covenant. Whether his actions were criminal will ultimately be for others to decide.

"But what he did was without a doubt unconstitutional. It was unpatriotic. And it was fundamentally un-American. And when he used the power of his Presidency to put the enormous pressure on state, local — and local elections officials and his own Vice President, it became downright dangerous.

"On January 6th that pressure became deadly.

"Ruby Freeman said the President is supposed to protect every American, not target them. And she is right. If the most powerful person in the world can bring the full weight of the Presidency down on an ordinary citizen who is merely doing her job with a lie as big and heavy as a mountain, who among us is safe?

"None of us is. None of us. In city councils and town councils, on school boards and election boards, from the Congress to the courts, dedicated public servants are leaving their posts because of death threats to them and to their families. This is not who we are. It must not become who we are.

"Our democracy held because courageous people like those you heard from today put their oath to the Constitution above their loyalty to one man or to one party.

"The system held, but barely. And the question remains, will it hold again? If we are able to communicate anything during these hearings, I hope it is this: we have been blessed beyond measure to live in the world's greatest democracy.

"That is a legacy to be proud of and to cherish. But it is not one to be taken for granted.

"That we have lived in a democracy for more than 200 years does not mean we shall do so tomorrow. We must reject violence. We must embrace our Constitution with the reverence it deserves, take our oath of office and duties as citizens seriously, informed by the knowledge of right and wrong, and armed with no more than the power of our ideas and the truth carry on this venerable experiment in self-governance.

"Thank you, Mr. Chairman. And I yield back."

Bennie Thompson: "Without objection, the Chair recognizes the gentlewoman from Wyoming, Ms. Cheney, for a closing statement."

Liz Cheney: "Thank you very much, Mr. Chairman. Lady Ruby and Shaye, thank you for your courage. Thank you for your strength. Thank you for — for being here today. It — it means so much for everyone to hear your story. So thank you for that. We have had tremendous testimony today. We've been reminded that we're a nation of laws.

"And we've been reminded by you and by Speaker Bowers and Secretary of State Raffensperger and Mr. Sterling that our institutions don't defend themselves. Individuals do that. And we've reminded that it takes public servants. It takes people who've made a commitment to our system to defend our system. We also have been reminded what it means to take an oath under God to the Constitution, what it means to defend the Constitution.

"And we were reminded by Speaker Bowers that our Constitution is indeed a divinely inspired document. And so it's been an honor to spend time with you and with our previous witnesses here today. To date, more than 30 witnesses called before this committee have not done what you've done, but have invoked their Fifth Amendment rights against self-incrimination.

"Roger Stone took the fifth. General Michael Flynn took the fifth. John Eastman took the fifth. Others like Steve Bannon and Peter Navarro simply refused to comply with lawful subpoenas. And they have been indicted. Mark Meadows has hidden behind President Trump's claims of executive privilege and immunity from subpoenas.

"We're engaged now in litigation with Mr. Meadows. The American people in our hearings have heard from Bill Barr, Jeff Rosen, Richard Donoghue, and many others who stood up and did what is right. And they will hear more of that testimony soon. But the American people have not yet heard from Mr. Trump's former White House counsel, Pat Cipollone.

"Our committee is certain that Donald Trump does not want Mr. Cipollone to testify here. Indeed our evidence shows that Mr. Cipollone and his office tried to do what was right. They tried to stop a number of President Trump's plans for January 6th. Today and in our coming hearings you will hear testimony from other Trump White House staff explaining what Mr. Cipollone said and did including on January 6th. But we think the American people deserve to hear from Mr. Cipollone personally.

"He should appear before this committee, and we are working to secure his testimony. Thank you, Mr. Chairman. I yield back."

Bennie Thompson: "People answer the call to public service in such different ways. Some run for office. Some volunteer to make sure that neighbors can get to their voting locations. Some work at polling sites to help Election Day go smoothly. Some look into problems to guarantee our elections are secure and accurate, just to name a few.

"As I mentioned at the start of this hearing, when we talk about our democratic institutions we are talking about these individuals and many others who do these jobs across the country. They represent the backbone of our democracy at its most important moments: when the citizens cast their votes and when those votes are counted.

"We've heard the stories of their courage. They've earned the thanks of a grateful nation. But for Donald Trump, these witnesses and others like them were another roadblock to his attempt to cling to power. On Thursday, we'll hear about another part of that scheme, his attempt to corrupt the — the country's top law enforcement body, the Justice Department, to support his attempt to overturn the election.

"Just as we heard today that Donald Trump was deeply involved in a scheme to pressure state officials to overturn the election results, we'll hear — we will hear on Thursday that Donald Trump was also the driving force behind the effort to corrupt the Justice Department. Listen to this clip from the former Acting Attorney General Richard Donoghue."

[multimedia]

Richard Donoghue: "**The President said suppose I do this. Suppose I replace him, Jeff Rosen, with him, Jeff Clark. What do you do? And I said Sir, I would resign immediately. There is no way I'm serving one minute under this guy, Jeff Clark.**"

Bennie Thompson: "You'll hear from Mr. Donoghue in person on Thursday as my colleague Mr. Kinzinger presents details about this plan. The Chair requests those in the hearing room remain seated until the Capitol Police have escorted members from the room. Without objection the committee stands adjourned."

# # #

Made in the USA
Columbia, SC
16 March 2023

13899112R00046